A CLEARING IN THE WOODS

A CLEARING IN THE WOODS

CREATING CONTEMPORARY GARDENS

ROGER FOLEY

THE MONACELLI PRESS

To my family: Darcy, Kate, and Molly. More beautiful
and surprising than any garden could be, they are my heart's
clearing in the woods.

Copyright © 2009 The Monacelli Press, a division
of Random House, Inc.
Photographs copyright © 2009 Roger Foley

Published in the United States by The Monacelli Press,
a division of Random House, Inc.
1745 Broadway, New York, New York 10019

The Monacelli Press and colophon are trademarks
of Random House, Inc.

Library of Congress Cataloging-in-Publication Data

Foley, Roger.
A clearing in the woods : creating contemporary gardens /
Roger Foley. — 1st ed.
p. cm.
ISBN 978-1-58093-245-5
1. Gardens—Design. 2. Landscape gardening.
3. Landscape photography. I. Title.
SB473.F655 2009
712'.6—dc22   2009020789

Printed in China

10 9 8 7 6 5 4 3 2 1
First edition

Designed by Susan Evans, Design Per Se, Inc.

www.monacellipress.com

CONTENTS

INTRODUCTION

Landscape pictures offer us, I think, three verities—geography, autobiography, and metaphor. Geography is, if taken alone, sometimes boring, autobiography is frequently trivial, and metaphor can be dubious. But taken together . . . the three kinds of information strengthen each other and reinforce what we all work to keep intact—an affection for life.

—Robert Adams, "Truth and Landscape"

My introduction to landscape photography was through my grandfather Max Rubin, a serious amateur whose black-and-white landscapes hung in our home. But it wasn't until I spent my sophomore year of college in France that I first saw the landscape as a subject for self-expression. I fell in love with the work of the Impressionists first hand, spending many hours at the Jeu de Paume museum in Paris, standing transfixed in front of those paintings. I felt as if I could absorb the energy from the light rendered through their brushstrokes. These paintings taught me an exciting way to see light and color in the landscape and through their influence, heightened the sensual experience of being in the natural world. And then, the following year, *The Creation* by Ernst Haas was published. In the pages of that seminal book, which translated the Book of Genesis into dazzling color photographs, I understood how my intense response to the Impressionists could be translated into photography where subject, form, light, and color all work together to transform the act of recording into the art of seeing.

And so I became a photographer. At first my landscape pictures were limited to personal work, where I had the freedom to chose my own subjects: forests, mountain streams, tropical islands, and ancient Asian vistas. To earn a living, I photographed for a variety of companies until I discovered garden photography and realized I could bring the personal and professional together. Since then, I've been fortunate to spent most of my time in gardens.

Garden photography is not for anyone in a hurry. It works best when you slow down and look and look, and then look some more. All this looking serves as an examining and a cataloging of the physical materials, where they are in the landscape, and what the photographic possibilities may be. It's only when the objective *looking* turns into the subjective *seeing* that a beautiful garden photograph can be made. The seeing of a picture signals an understanding of the spirit of a place, where light and form are distilled through the camera in such a way as to persuade viewers into believing that in a two-dimensional mapping of bits of color on a page, they can feel what it's like to inhabit that space.

To find these moments, you must stay open to being inspired, often by something unexpected. Early morning fog can change your plans for dramatic low-angled sunlight glinting off a landscape, but it can reward you with moody, pastel scenes that impart a timeless quality to

7

a garden. Often, there will be a moment when a scene snaps into focus—when all of the elements come together to express something special about the sensation of being in this place at this moment. The most successful photographs will speak to the viewer in an intuitive language, bypassing the head and going straight to the heart. Then the viewer will experience the sounds, scents, and textures of nature heightened by the rhythms of repeated colors and shapes and by the patterns etched out of light and shadow. At that moment, when the photograph changes from a window to a door, the viewer becomes the visitor.

Translating the colors of nature through the photography medium is tricky. To most people, it would probably seem too simple to worry about. Beautiful gardens full of colorful plants: what could be easier to photograph? But most gardens are predominately green, and while the eyes of a visitor can easily discern the layers of green architecture—tree lines, mixed borders of shrubs and perennials that transition down to lawns and grass paths—the single eye of a camera has no depth perception. Having only two dimensions to work with, the photograph must give the illusion of volume, space, and distance through the use of perspective and by taking advantage of the powerful effects of light and shadow.

Out in the garden, light is always changing, and during the magical hours when the sun is low on the horizon, those changes accelerate. The general course of sunlight through the garden can be predicted, of course, but the subtle effects of the light—exactly where late-day shafts will fall to reveal the texture of a stone wall, or when the early morning sun will clear a tree line and light up a hillside of flowering crabapples—must be seen in the moment to understand how they will transform a landscape.

In the wrong light, attempts at garden photography can fall short. Light that is too flat can melt shapes together until they lose their sense of volume. Light that's too hard makes the garden seem brittle and fragmented with glaring highlights and opaque shadows. But early morning rays of sun will outline a bank of flowering shrubs, separating them from the dark hillside behind and creating a sense of foreground and background. Softer directional light adds a graduated shading to the cylindrical shapes of trees and shrubs to suggest their volume. And late-day sun draws long, broad shadows of trees across a lawn that read as lines of perspective as they recede into the distance.

Garden photography involves the art of being a translator, someone who conveys not only the literal facts in front of the lens, but also the sense and meaning of what's being expressed there. It is my goal to respond to the ideas and emotions that I find in a well-conceived garden, rather than imposing any predetermined formulas. Each garden assignment becomes a process of rein-vention, starting anew in how I respond to light and form. I don't want to simply show that a low retaining wall separates the tame, clipped lawn from the wild, textured meadow beyond it. I want to reveal how the character of one side intensifies the experience of seeing the other with the low wall acting as a firm hand, keeping the two worlds apart.

I hope that readers of this book will come away with a growing appreciation for the creative work of the talented landscape design practitioners featured here, and that they will find some insights into the creative process and the many paths that are taken to design satisfying gardens. More ambitious than that is a hope that readers may be inspired to become more keenly aware of the splendor found in beautiful gardens where the natural world invites us in to a sanctuary where we belong. The yearning for this connection is what inspires people to commission gardens, to design gardens, and to photograph them. The act of capturing this alchemy, where light and air mix with plants, dirt, stone, and wood to create something more than the sum of its parts is the reason why we do what we do.

This desire for a clearing in the woods, a place to explore the pleasures of nature, is so important for us that it is one definition of paradise. For me, that feeling of being secluded in one's own space, away from the chaos of the world, provides me first with a sense of serenity and later a feeling of rediscovery. It is that rediscovery of the natural world that creates what landscape photographer Robert Adams described as "an affection for life." I've tried to capture that in my photography and now I offer it here for the readers of this book, who, I hope, will become the "visitors" of these gardens.

Robert Adams, "Truth and Landscape" *Beauty in Photography: Essays in Defense of Traditional Values* (New York: Aperture, Inc., 1981), p. 14.

FARRAR POND GARDEN

Massachusetts   Mikyoung Kim, Mikyoung Kim Design

Think of the fence as a skeleton that ripples over the sinuous contours of the forested property, tumbling up and down sloped hillsides, bending through groves of birches. That's what Mikyoung Kim designed to meet a set of priorities that included both protecting a view of Farrar Pond and enclosing a side yard for her clients' German Shepard. Kim, who has a background in music and sculpture, created an organic fence by stitching it into the landscape using the pickets of the fence to create a visual rhythm.

Composed of thousands of bars of steel, the fence is woven together using a system of hinged joints that allow it to expand or contract in relationship to the topography. The bars are layered four across, creating a foot-deep barrier; Cor-Ten steel was selected for its rust-colored patina that mimics the soft, darker tones in nature. "When it's scrunched up it becomes dense, but when it's completely open it feels transparent," says Kim.

Like all great landscapes, the site dictated many of the choices. Magenta-colored rhododendron and flowering trees were removed to keep the landscape more in tune with a native Eastern forest. Oaks, birches, and eastern white pines were added. A path of pervious lilac bluestone pavers, laid out in a field of moss, meanders down the slope, becoming more scattered in pattern as they reach the perimeter, reminiscent of the fallen birch trees in the forest. In the front entry, Kim established a more formal rhythm, and she substituted a low-growing sedum for the moss to handle the heating system beneath the paving that melts the snow in winter.

The koi pond, designed with a sleek and modern sensibility, is an abstract translation of the natural pond in the distance. Wave-textured glass and curved grillwork of laminated stainless steel are used for the bridges and walkways, creating a translucency that brings immediacy to the water below while enhancing the visibility of the fish.

Even when most gardens look washed-out in the mid-day sun, the trunks of the trees and the ribs of the fence offer stark shadow patterns across the bluestone pavers. "In winter, the context can become a white canvas with vertical vertebrae," says Kim. "In the fall the fence becomes one of the elements of color between the yellows and the vibrant reds of the foliage."

FARRAR POND

13

CHILMARK HOUSE GARDEN

Martha's Vineyard, Massachusetts   Steve Stimson, Steve Stimson Associates

"It really does look like a whale coming up out of the little bluestem grass," says Steve Stimson of the enormous boulder that sits inches away from this modern one-story house on the leeward end of Martha's Vineyard. The stone, one of many "glacial erratics" on the island, was deposited here from the receding glacier long ago, and both architects Olson Sundberg Kundig Allen and Stimson thought it was fine right where it was. The house was built around it and the courtyard garden at the entrance was designed to maximize its presence.

This treatment says a lot about the way Stimson thinks about a site: "We are trying to extend the spaces of the house out into the landscape so we do respond to the architecture, but I think we have a responsibility to make that link back to the site. Our landscape should not be a man-made transition; it should have its own connection to the broader landscape so that it belongs. Here, the geology and topography were clearly a big factor."

The play between what is man-made and what comes from nature can be seen most clearly in the back of the house where a long wall of windows looks out to the sea. Moving outside, there are a series of terraces made from concrete pavers manufactured with a smooth surface the color of parchment. Then the surface becomes more natural with an ample lawn to be used for play and entertaining. The lawn ends in a long, low wall made of cut granite, the only type of stone used on the property and one that evokes the hand-worked stone on stone barns and foundations on the island.

This wall marks the transition from the practical, tame outdoor spaces into a more natural landscape, a shift in grade into a meadow full of native plants. Midway through the meadow there is a short length of stone wall, which echoes back to the low wall at the edge of the lawn, and then out to the sea and the horizon line.

The respect for the natural landscape is most evident in the way the existing trees on the site were carefully protected and reverentially treated in the native plantings designed around them. "Saving trees is much more important than planting trees, especially in this landscape," says Stimson. "We find on these island projects that it takes a minimum of five years for trees to establish and they never really look like they're native. It's really hard to make a tree look like it belongs there because of the wind conditions."

17

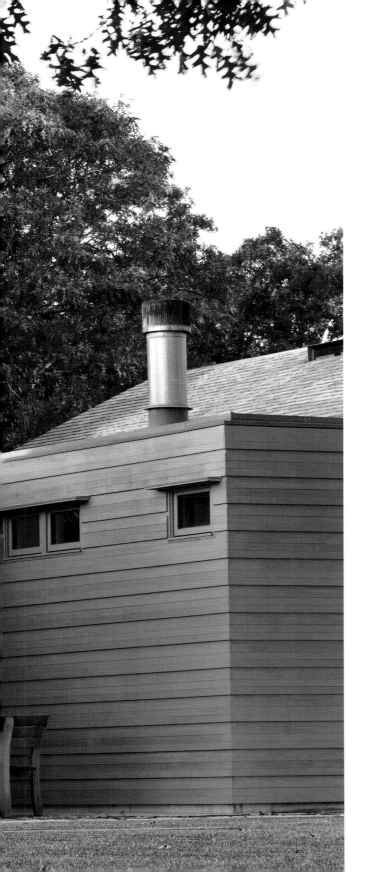

CHILMARK HOUSE GARDEN

LONGHOUSE RESERVE

East Hampton, New York   Jack Lenor Larsen

"I feel strongly that museums, generally, can't compete with the out-of-doors when it comes to sculpture," says textile designer Jack Lenor Larsen. "Usually sculpture is hard and nature is soft so the contrast is becoming." And then there's the light that moves across surfaces, changing from hour to hour and from one season to the next. To see a familiar sculpture in a new light is a daily reality for Larsen, not a cliché.

Larsen has always been an artist who elevates collecting to an art itself. His house and sculpture garden are now LongHouse Reserve, a non-profit public organization that promotes living with art in all its forms, which is what he's been doing himself since the 1960s. Even with its higher purpose, it's still Larsen's garden. He has a dune garden that recalls the Kröller-Müller sculpture garden near Amsterdam, which impressed him years ago. There is a large pond near the house, where he recently had a summer's night birthday dinner for fourteen on a large platform floating amid the lotus and water lilies. "Buckminster Fuller's daughter saw us putting up a tent in the wind—we were having trouble—and suggested a dome instead." Now Fuller's Fly's Eye Dome is a looming presence in the garden.

Over the years, much of the landscape has been carefully transformed into backdrops for the ever-changing sculpture collection. Larsen, with his weaver's sensibility, has defined quiet, richly textured garden rooms made from native trees, conifers, shrubs, and grasses that create secluded spaces where the art can be seen to best advantage. The garden is interlaced with walking paths, cool under tall trees that connect to clearings and meadows. But in this garden when a curve in a path reveals a clearing, there's likely to be a very large sculpture there.

The composition is always changing. Larsen delights in the discovery of a new spot for a sculpture that will enhance the viewing experience. And outdoors, there is the dimension of time. "Within the seasons, things change and the natural foliage grows. And sometimes we clear it away," Larsen says. "We keep thinking that if we add something, it will solve the situation and make a piece glow, but it's often removing the competition that does the trick. I'm learning that subtraction is the key to elegance."

27

28

LONGHOUSE RESERVE

LONGHOUSE RESERVE

EAST HAMPTON GARDEN

Long Island, New York   Edwina von Gal, Edwina von Gal & Co.

"My goal is always to make people acutely aware of the beauty of the basic elements of nature," says Edwina von Gal. "How do you make people notice the bark on a tree? How do you get them to just stop a second, to see the way the root flare is at the bottom of the trunk?" Von Gal does it by paring away everything unnecessary or ornamental, until the landscape contains a minimum of elements that take on added importance in the simplicity of the design.

"I need to start with the plan," she explains. "I go and mark it out, look at it, and then I go back to the plan, mark it out again. It can continue to evolve until the day we do it. It's about scale." That intuitive process—how much lawn, the height of a stone wall, where should the trees go—ultimately produces a landscape of quiet power where the broad lawn, outlined by the thin line of a low stone wall and adorned with a simple stepping stone path, leads the eye through the yard and down the gentle slope to the pool and pond.

The weathered-gray house speaks the same minimalist language as the quiet twelve-acre garden. Where there is seasonal interest and color, it is designed as a discovery to be found behind a shrub hedge or around the bend of a path, like the formal cutting garden, with its lush late summer shades of indigo, mauve and orange. This vivid border is separated from the main house by a coarse lawn planted with an orchard of Yoshino cherry trees, their deeply textured bark on thick trunks mottled with lichen. The gray of the tree bark and the green of the lichen echo von Gal's minimalist color palette: the grays of the architecture and fieldstone against the greens of the lawns and shrub borders.

Von Gal avoids large elements of hardscaping: "The idea is not to draw attention to that because you have nature and you have architecture. You don't really need another voice." Most paths here are mown grass, like the one running through the vast panicum (switch grass) meadow behind the house. That meadow covers a hillside that has been carefully graded to accentuate a feeling of looking up from the bottom of the hill—not a small accomplishment in an area as flat as the Hamptons. In the summer with all those grasses, she says, "The meadow exhales—it gives the whole place a subliminal shimmer."

EAST HAMPTON GARDEN

37

EAST HAMPTON GARDEN

EAST HAMPTON GARDEN

42

EAST HAMPTON GARDEN

THE ROHDIE GARDEN

Ulster County, New York   Dean Riddle, Dean Riddle Gardens

"If there is anything in the world that teaches you patience, it's a garden," says Dean Riddle. "With a garden you can knock yourself out and give it everything you can, but then you have to stand back and let nature take its course." It is the art of watching a garden unfold over years that "lets the garden itself start to speak its name," to reach that "otherness you can't quite put your finger on," he explains.

Clients Barbara and Bob Rohdie have relished the journey. They knew what they wanted for their eleven-acre Catskill mountain retreat: a lush perennial garden situated between their contemporary house and a dazzling blue pool positioned downhill in a sunny, natural bowl. Beginning at the top of a hillside covered with rock and rubble, Riddle started at the guesthouse, where he planted a leafy border along the facade to help tie the structure to the site. Densely planted with deciduous shrubs, such as ninebark, smoke bush, and hydrangea, the raised bed is contained by native Catskill boulders clothed with Virginia creeper. A broken-stone patio, fanning out from the stones, further anchored the house and created a plateau-like landing to view the garden, pool, and a curtain of dappled Japanese willows beyond.

"The hillside was always going to be about getting to and from the pool," says Riddle. But he did not want the steps to seem rigid or purposeful: "I wanted it to feel more like meandering there and back." Using stones collected on the property, Riddle made three broad, descending terraces bisected by a steppingstone path that allows a gentle decent. Along the path are narrow, alternating drifts of drought-tolerant perennials, which are woven together throughout the terraces. By repeating blues, pinks, and yellows, he created waves of color from May through October. Among these are 'Blue Fortune' hyssop, salvia, 'Ruby Giant' echinacea, and Russian sage. As accents Riddle placed pots of Cordyline 'Red Star' with its spiky reddish-purple sword-shaped leaves on terrace walls.

The pool deck is furnished with a vivid blue, Wharton Esherick–inspired "Boomerang" bench. At the back edge of the pool is a row of 'Limelight' hydrangea. At the entrance to the pool, Riddle laid rectangular stone pavers among river stones, and planted them with dwarf boxwoods waiting for the self-sown perilla and Verbena bonariensis to spring up later between the stones. Now, in the third year, even some native Queen Anne's lace has crept from the woods into nooks and crannies. The hardwood forest beside the property has been thinned, so "in subtle ways we are painting the woods," he says, opening them up to give deeper views within.

"What has made this garden possible is the Rohdies' willingness to open their property to me, to let me learn it as I go," says Riddle. "They've made me feel like I could treat it as a piece of art that's ongoing, that I can constantly tweak and fine tune."

45

THE ROHDIE GARDEN

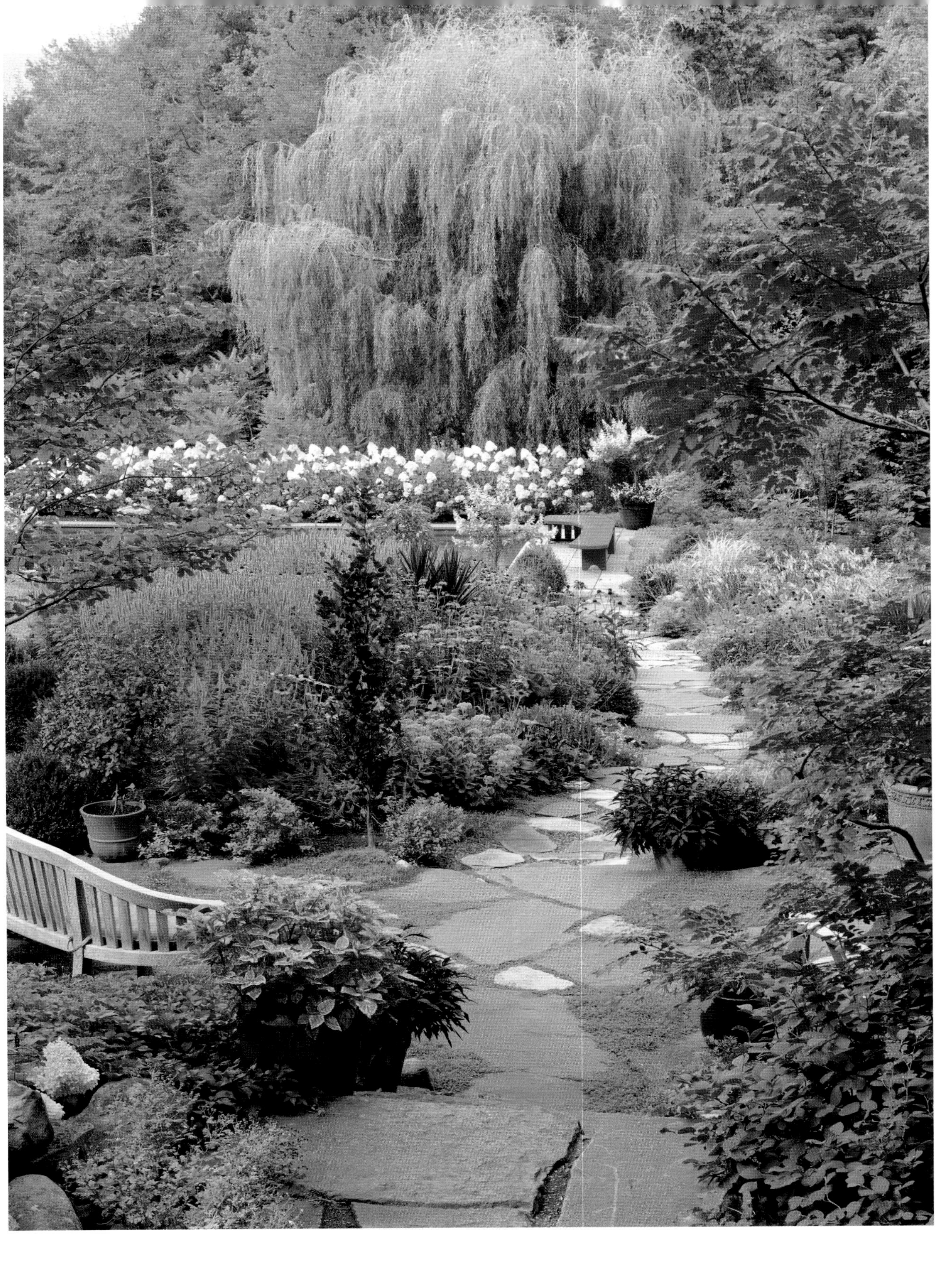

SHAKER MODERN GARDEN

Greenwich, Connecticut   Bruce Eckerson, Wesley Stout Associates

What Bruce Eckerson wanted to create in this Connecticut landscape was a Shaker garden with a modern twist, where form follows function and "where all the details are boiled down to the bare minimum." Taking cues from the plain-faced, white clapboard house, Eckerson chose time-less materials—granite and rough-hewn wood—that were pared down to emphasize their essential character in a landscape layered with a green plant palette.

Reclaimed Connecticut granite curbing became a metaphor for the whole project. Quarried more than two hundred years ago, the old stone was used to offset a new fabricated thermal granite cut to have rock-faced edges and smooth surfaces. The clean and neat cut of the stone reflected the quality of Shaker workmanship in that it has a "very simple, very spare look that has to be done beautifully," says Eckerson. The choice of a consistent material in the garden walls, terraces, and walkways provides a harmonious background in a garden that moves seamlessly from one outdoor space to another.

The granite and other materials also juxtapose the old with the new—the clean line of the stain-less-steel railings running opposite the gnarly living fence of espaliered apple trees, for example. "In every transition and in every detail there is a sense of a contrast," adds Eckerson. "The front is very spare; the back is more elaborate." The tension between traditional and modern is seen in the rustic cedar gate that opens upon a sleek modern koi pond. Linking the house and the garage, this narrow pond establishes "a vertical dialogue between the two gables that is refracted through the koi pond."

51

That duality continues into a dining court where modern furniture—a simple table with yolk-yellow chairs—is framed by low boxwood hedges against a weeping wall of water. Four linden trees anchor the corners and create a green canopy. To give each of the garden rooms its own identity and to lead to the next, Eckerson layered them into each other in a roughly diagonal fashion. A cantilevered staircase ascends a nine-foot change in grade from the dining room to a pool and an outdoor living room with a large fireplace.

Since the original clients didn't want a surfeit of color in the garden, Eckerson limited the plant palette to blues, greens, and whites and repeated certain plants—boxwood, hollies, hemlocks and hydrangeas—to enclose spaces within richly textures walls of foliage. To add contrast, he placed espaliered apple trees against Norway spruce and to create drama, he chose parrotia trees for their low-hanging, muscular branches to hide the entrance into the property. He interrupted the front of the three-bay detached garage by interspersing Japanese maples against the stone veneer between the doors. Circles of clipped hollies, spaced evenly, dot the front of the house without ever suggesting there is a sophisticated, interlocking series of spaces beyond the garden gate.

SHAKER MODERN GARDEN

SHAKER MODERN GARDEN

MEADOW GARDEN

Long Island, New York   Michael Blake, Wild At Heart

Dunes set the stage in this naturalistic garden on Gardiner's Bay in the Hamptons. Michael Blake chose hair grass, broom sedge, and American beach grass to blanket most of the slope, knowing the grasses would protect the dunes and would bring a unifying scheme into the garden. To accentuate paths wending their way up the high bluff, he planted bearberry, a creeping evergreen ground cover, on the tops of the hummocks. Shrubs of rosa rugosa and bayberry were cleared off the dunes and replanted on the perimeter to open and frame the view from the house.

The grove of stunted white, scarlet, and post oaks on top of the ridge is a gift of time. "Only something that grows from a seed over the course of sixty years can grow up and live there," Blake explains. Closer to the house, he moved away from the wild to more formal elements, including a koi pond and drifts of Russian sage, white cosmos, 'Longwood Blue' caryopteris, and flag iris on the bottom of the hill. "We wanted to have something wistful, with movement that played off the grassy nature on the dunes," he says. Playing off the cylindrical shapes of the house, designed by BarnesCoy Architects, a circle-shaped lawn was added with a looping path that leads under the half-arch of a ruin folly.

Behind the house are a pool, a play lawn, and a mowed grass path leading out to a fifteen-acre conservation meadow. The path links the ordered parts of the garden with the informal meadow, where Blake incorporated deer-resistant plants such as salvias, lavenders, panicum, and Hakonechloa grass. A stand of cherry trees and bayberries blocks the view of a neighboring house and gives the meadow a sense of scale. Blake cut down some dead trees and used the stumps as benches, chairs, and tables to create seating areas throughout the property. "I always wanted to use slabs of trees trunks in landscapes as outdoor furniture," he explains.

59

MEADOW GARDEN

MEADOW GARDEN

MOUNT SHARON FARM

Orange County, Virginia   Charles Stick, Charles Stick, Inc.

The owners of this historic landscape in the Piedmont region of Virginia asked two landscape architects for a garden plan. The first bluntly insisted that all the boxwood be cut down. The second, Charles Stick, studied the 450-foot-long allée and concluded, "The old hedge was part of the joy and the genius of the place."

With its central spine as a grand hallway, the American boxwood provided a way to link the 1930s Georgian-revival brick house through a garden that sloped up a hill. Once inside its 20-foot-tall living walls, the tunnel-like shape would work to conceal and then reveal a series of garden rooms, each room with its own character.

The first and the largest room is a classical rose garden that extends down four terraces of formal parterres. Two pergolas smothered in roses sit at the top; below two pavilions overlook a yew-enclosed rose garden also known also as the "Garden of Four Seasons" after its Italian statuary. The last terrace has a fountain in the middle of a lush green lawn that slopes off into the surrounding countryside. A black walnut and two tulip poplars bracketing the space define the spatial limits of the ambitious rose garden.

Emerging at the end of the eighty-year-old hedge is a *tapis vert* garden bordered by a row of clipped hornbeam, a staple in traditional French gardens. Next, a brick path leads to a garden with a double perennial border that winds its way to the Ellipse Pavilion, a recreation of a Chinese Chippendale–style pavilion that once graced the site of George Mason's birthplace, Gunston Hall. "At the end of the garden, the shape of the opening framed a view out into infinity," says Stick.

67

Stick chose a restrained plant palette and low-maintenance ground covers, such as the liriope for the parterre slopes. As he sees it, he provided the architectural bones for his clients so they could "paint whatever picture they wanted within that framework." And, remembering Thomas Jefferson's words, "Shade is our Elysium," Stick built pavilions and pergolas to ensure that the garden and its varying views can be enjoyed during the hot and humid months.

That view of the Virginia countryside, of farms, ponds, and low, rolling hills was Stick's touchstone for what felt right in this design. Fountains, a pavilion, a path and an octagonal terrace were all placed to draw the eye out to reference the lovely agricultural landscape. And much was subtracted to avoid interfering with the views. "When you look at great sculptures, artists take a piece of stone and then take something away from it to bring it to life," he says. That principle applies to simplifying the landscape to reveal the essential, "If you plant the right trees in the right place or put a walkway to emphasize a view, that is what's going to outlast us all."

MOUNT SHARON FARM

MOUNT SHARON FARM

MOUNT SHARON FARM

74

JOSEPH E. ROBERT GARDEN

Virginia   Guy Morgan Williams, DCA Landscape Architects

In this park-like, historic estate preserving the pastoral "sense of place" was paramount. The existing centuries-old oaks created a scale of grandeur with their expansive canopy, but to design a mature garden that felt like it had been there forever meant developing a sense of proportion. Keeping the largest trees intact, Williams subtracted much of the overgrown middle canopy to open up views to the house and across the lawns so the landscape felt endless. Along the new drive, he added more trees to a run of Yoshino cherries to draw visitors in and up a hill to the 1920s fieldstone house, framing it and the new cobblestone entry circle with its contorted, cut-leaf maples.

The mature plant material was used to sequence and then delineate spaces. Sweeps of existing plants were grouped to more clearly define existing garden rooms, such as the cloak of 'Nikko Blue' hydrangeas that ring the koi pond or the mass of reclaimed azaleas that surround the hammock. The goal is for everything to look established, but, as Williams explains, "A garden changes every year and new things are added and these changes alter other things." It is the art of balancing the tension between letting nature be and knowing when to rein nature back in that creates a garden that feels as though it has been there forever, untouched by man.

To give a new tennis court an old-world atmosphere, Williams built a twenty-foot high stone wall with ivy growing in arched panels and a hedge of clipped hornbeam on top. A small wrought iron Juliet balcony allows a peek into the court from above; spectators watch matches from the shaded semi-circular pergola swathed in roses, clematis, and climbing hydrangea. Built of rough-hewn wood steamed to produce an elegant curve, the construction is age old, with no nails— just pegs, posts, and beams. Timeless materials and techniques, such as the tennis-court wall laid in Endless Mountain stone using a semi-dry technique to minimize the joints, creates a sense of age. That attention to detail is evident in the courtside planting, where Williams wrapped the hardscaping in green from the weeping willows spilling into the court to the ivy-covered panels. The result is a cool, refreshing sanctuary.

But nature is ultimately in control in this eight-acre garden. When a grand tree falls in a storm, it will be missed. But, William says, "All of a sudden you have this sun in a spot you did not have it before," Having been fortunate to work on this garden for fifteen years, he has a vision of what will happen to it in fifty. Of course, being adaptable is key: "Some of the things that happen create new opportunities that are even better than what you thought you wanted to do."

JOSEPH E. ROBERT GARDEN

JOSEPH E. ROBERT GARDEN

HIGHLAND SPRING

Middleburg, Virginia   Donna Hackman

Donna Hackman has spent twenty years sculpting her three-acre garden room-by-room and path-by-path on a farmstead overlooking the Blue Ridge Mountains. It is a process of continual editing and re-evalution, where bulbs, perennials, shrubs, and trees are planted, relocated or removed, to create a more vibrant effect. Early in the process, Hackman recognized the value of the majestic hundred-year-old white oaks on her site that now provide a long-established look throughout the garden rooms and winding paths, evoking the classic English country gardens she admires.

She first addressed the more formal features around the Federal-style country house: the sunken garden, spring garden with a fountain, a clipped crabapple allée, and a clematis and rose-covered pergola. Next, she started clearing out the understory of the wooded site to reveal the under-lying architecture of the natural landscape, adding paths or a few steps here or there, but for the most part, allowing the downward slope of the hill from the house to dictate her design choices.

Taking cues from the landscape, a natural rock outcropping became the site for the primula and forget-me-not stream garden tumbling down the hill from a spring house in gently cascading waterfalls to a stepping-stone pond and a weeping Katsura tree. Nearby, a dining terrace was positioned half way down the slope, its curved front edge made of Virginia field stones found in the surrounding woods. Its floor was built up over one long winter from composting grass clippings, leaves, and top soil, layer after layer.

87

In the upper garden, visible from the house, a long rectangular lawn is enclosed by exuberant English-style borders twelve feet deep and one hundred fifty feet long, backed by dark green hemlock hedges. The borders are bisected by paths, creating four quadrants, each designed with a layered plant palette to showcase a different color theme through three seasons of interest. To strengthen this design with more structure, she added small trees and shrubs so that over time the ratio of flowers and bulbs would become equal to the trees and shrubs. After the first flush of the May/June bloom in the white border, for example, there are joyous clouds of allium, foxglove, and peonies mixed in with a deutzia and a variegated willow which provides nine months of pleasure.

Recently, the adjacent woodlands beyond the garden fence have been brought into focus by clearing out the tangle and planting spring bulbs and understory shrubs so that the garden now slowly fades into the surrounding woods. After working year-round from dawn to dusk, Hackman has no plans to stop expanding and fine-tuning her garden. When she comes in each evening, she knows, "My heart is out there with the garden."

88

HIGHLAND SPRING

HIGHLAND SPRING

A GEORGETOWN GARDEN

Washington, D.C.   William Morrow, William Morrow Garden Design, Inc.

When William Morrow began to work on his garden, he could hardly see the space for a forest of gigantic Southern Magnolias. "They are wonderful trees from a distance," he says, but he removed all but one from behind his 1890s brick townhouse to make room for a jubilant garden that would need sun to flourish.

The garden is only 5,000 square feet, but Morrow knew creating strong boundaries would make the space seem larger. One of the magnolias remains at the back as a screen and a structural barrier. Morrow also painted a seven-foot-high fence that bordered the yard on three sides a glossy black to help it disappear and to make the climbing roses—'Rambling Rector,' 'Fourth of July,' and 'Sombreuil'—pop out against a dark background.

To create the illusion of even more space, Morrow created an architectural layout of three terraces, each separated by low stone retaining walls with two steps up to the next level. "I wanted strong symmetry that bought order and definition to the spaces," he says. In each of them, the hard-scaping and plant material vary to accentuate purpose. In the entertaining area, there is wrought-iron seating and a faux-bois trough planted with kitchen herbs. A water-garden fountain with a simple spigot provides a focal point in the middle terrace. And in the upper garden, the shape of the path along the lavish English border suggests strolling. Pea gravel was used instead of grass because Morrow believes that grass is impractical in small urban yards because of the high maintenance to keep it lush.

The strolling garden is inspired by English perennial borders, but Morrow prefers bolder, brasher plants. Instead of planting a low hedge of boxwood to define the beds, he chose 'Crimson Pygmy' barberry, which added "a jolt of bright fire-engine red." To balance the profusion of combinations of perennials and bulbs, he repeated the dwarf barberry borders and added Irish yew within the beds for vertical interest. He also introduced plants reminiscent of his childhood, such as mayapples and Jack-in-the-Pulpits, but in the more exotic forms of rare Asian varieties.

Pots are used throughout the garden as strong structural statements. A pair planted with varie-gated agaves flanks the first set of steps; others surround the simple water feature. A space that includes every growing condition from shade to full sun, the garden has become a perfect test garden for plants. His rule of thumb for his client's gardens: "If a plant needs to be coddled, don't bother. It's much better to be cutting a plant back because it's so vigorous."

A GEORGETOWN GARDEN

A GEORGETOWN GARDEN

RUNNING CEDAR

Orlean, Virginia   Richard Arentz, Arentz Landscape Architects

The first winter, Richard Arentz hiked the eighty-five wooded acres of his property, studied U.S. Geologic Survey maps, and ultimately selected a fairly level site to build on, with its southern edge high above a bend in Virginia's Rappahannock River. He was building this house and garden for himself, but with the freedom of being his own client came the added responsibility to get it just right. The garden at Running Cedar, named for a local woodland ground cover, shows the hand of someone who has completely considered every detail of his man-made environment, while also staying in tune with the surrounding natural landscape.

His idea was to have a perfect marriage of house and garden where the outside flowed in through the house and the inside flowed out into the landscape. He and architect Richard Williams designed two country-style buildings of stucco and sheet metal surrounded by a garden with many traditional features of an English garden: a tree-lined allée, a belvedere, a formal courtyard, sweeping lawns, and a lush flower garden. But in this landscape, all elements are handled in a decidedly contemporary style: the functional geometry of straight paths against large, flat planes of lawn; the absence of any unnecessary ornamentation; and the materials themselves, in particular the stone, celebrated for their own beauty.

The connection to the river is most strongly felt in the entrance and front yard. Approaching the house from the parking court, the building itself is partially obscured by a high row of American boxwood. A paved walkway leads to a stone wall and the belvedere overlooking the river one hundred feet below. Here, to the right, is the first full view of the house, where a stone wall leads to the brick-red door and the sound of water. The river is out of earshot there so Arentz created an "allegorical river," as a metal trough juts out from the end of the wall and pours a thick stream of water into a deep basin at the threshold of the house.

Once inside, the stone wall continues through the foyer, living room, and dining room, leading out to a dramatic allée: two rows of matched 'Winter King' hawthorns under-planted with masses of 'White Lady' hellebores. Both plants are known for their uniform structure that fits the formal design, and their white flowers are in keeping with the garden's restrained color palette. Only as the grade steps down into the overflowing flower border at the west end of the garden are warm hues from butter yellow to brick red introduced. That same red is used on the front door, on all the outdoor seat cushions, and as a wall color in some rooms, reinforcing the flow between inside and outside. "It's about introducing a theme and sticking with it," says Arentz.

ORCHARD FARM

Potomac, Maryland   Sandra Clinton, Clinton & Associates

This garden has all the amenities of home—kitchen, dining room, living room, foyer, hallways—except the floor plan is open to the sky and the playroom has a vegetable garden with a compost heap. That's what Sandy Clinton designed—a home away from home—two hundred yards from her clients' 1830s farmhouse in Potomac, Maryland. "It was a unique opportunity to develop an entire story," says Clinton. In a series of sunken garden rooms, her clients, Gay and Tony Barclay, can "garden, pick vegetables, prepare a meal, dine, or just relax with a book."

Being out of sight from the encroaching suburban sprawl was paramount so the garden was sited down a hill four feet below grade. Clinton and Gay Barclay spent an afternoon positioning an Adirondack settee in different locations within the 4,500-square-foot space to optimize the rural views of paddock, corncribs, and pastures. Clinton quickly understood that the south-facing site would need shade (arbors), the sound of water (fountains), and plants to soften and ultimately cool the garden.

To develop a practical circulation system between the rooms, Clinton worked up a series of sketches, including a formal parterre design, but she knew what would best suit the Barclays' lifestyle would be one that incorporated the vernacular of a farm. Taking architectural suggestions from the outbuildings, she linked the slatted kitchen walls to a century-old corncrib by using recycled wood from a barn on the property and gave a nod to the reddish standing-seam roof of the farmhouse in the kitchen roof. In keeping with agricultural construction techniques, peeled locus trunks are the support posts for the arbors, and wood from the barn was also reused in the arbor beams, the potting shed, and the whimsical picket fence surrounding the dining room.

A small rose arbor draws visitors down into the garden, across the foyer to an alcove where the Adirondack settee, now painted a welcoming yellow, is placed. Two other freestanding shade structures anchor and enclose the living and dining rooms placed across a hallway from one another. A millstone fountain in the living room adds coolness to the space as water splashes over the edge and falls into the rocks below, and a farm well pump adds rustic charm to the modern kitchen. The last arbor is above the potting shed in the herb and raised-bed vegetable garden. Different paving materials—fieldstones, granite, cobbles, and brick—were used like scatter rugs to delineate the three main living spaces.

For a garden that receives sun from noon to sunset, Clinton added 'Heritage' river birch, viburnums, a fringe tree, and 'Natchez' crepe myrtles to provide more shade, and she planted 'Annabelle' hydrangeas and butterfly bush to soften the stone walls. During the summer months, clematis, Japanese wisteria, and climbing hydrangeas cover the arbors to provide a green roof. Each year, Gay Barclay, an avid gardener, adds new annuals, vegetables, and perennials to the mix.

ORCHARD FARM

110

ORCHARD FARM

FERRY COVE

Sherwood, Maryland   James van Sweden, Oehme, van Sweden & Associates, Inc.

Think of it as painting with plants with great masses of color that move and change depending on the wind, the weather, or the season. That's what James van Sweden intended when he designed this meadow garden to complement a complex of modern houses in Sherwood, Maryland, on the Chesapeake Bay. "We wanted large, free, informal drifts of grasses that resulted in a natural, relaxed, bold landscape," says van Sweden. And like most of the firm's gardens, this one would be low in maintenance and require no water once established. With a 250-foot set back from the Chesapeake, the meadow acts like a filter, cleaning run-off water before it reaches the bay.

The view through a sea of grasses is uninterrupted from the decks of the houses, which float amid fountain grass and silver-tinged mountain mint that hums with bees. The rest of the four-acre meadow, formerly a flat field of soybeans, is punctuated with tough trees and shrubs like bayberry, alder, crepe myrtle, and hackberry.

In designing the houses, architect and owner Suman Sorg drew inspiration from her native India and from the agricultural countryside of the Eastern Shore of Maryland. The buildings, with their barn-like roofs, are made of concrete block and sheets of marine plywood edged in steel. Instead of just one large house Sorg created a compound of three buildings linked by outdoor walkways that double as porches and vine-covered pergolas. All of these structures protect the back courtyard garden from the bay's harsh winds and punishing salt sprays.

115

This microclimate allowed van Sweden to use the exotics Sorg loved and to create more richly detailed plantings areas with layers of hot colored perennials, ranging from a low carpet of yellow coreopsis to the bold, vertical strokes of Rudbekia maxima. Masses of red shrub roses and deep burgundy daylilies provide a backdrop for the seating and outdoor dining areas, while the luxuriant blooms of a pink hibiscus mimic the shape of the circular pool. Van Sweden prefers black-bottomed pools for their pond-like appearance and their mystery.

"Our gardens reflect the unharnessed beauty of the landscape through the seasons," says van Sweden. Except for early spring when the meadow is mowed down, this landscape is always alive with wildlife, always surprising, and always changing as the color turns from greens to golds to browns. In winter, the garden becomes a line drawing with its dried stems, seed heads, stalks, and bare branches poking out from a white canvas of snow.

116

FERRY COVE

STONELEIGH FARM

Piedmont, Virginia   Donna Hackman

In this landscape of ponds, lush pastures, and hills folding back into native woodlands, Donna Hackman understood that great gardens are made when nature is heightened. But a light touch would be needed. The focus had to remain on opening up views and framing them from every possible vantage point. "You have to go with your site, what it calls for. It would have been a sin to close off that view," she says.

To expand the vista, a tennis court was removed from a berm above one of the ponds and a stand of straggly trees thinned to just one with character. Building retaining walls and linking them together with a series of steps solved the problem of how to move gracefully up and down the steep slope below the house. Along the walls, borders of bulbs, flowers, and shrubs—nepeta, geraniums, alliums, and 'Annabelle' hydrangeas—were planted to give a sense of romance. Sometimes the view was framed under a canopy of trees to give it a more intimate scale; other times the view was closed off momentarily to recreate a sense of discovery.

A pergola based on a design by the English architect Edwin Lutyens and garden designer Gertrude Jekyll was constructed to highlight sight lines and to provide a resting place. Honeysuckle, clematis, and roses climb up the steps and spill down the arbor, whose high arch frames the pond view between hand-hewn beams reclaimed from an old barn. The stone matches the original warm tones of the fieldstone from the pre–Civil War era house.

123

The pergola that shades the pool house terrace also serves as an entrance to the lawn or as an exit back up to the upper terrace lined with sitting walls. In an open landscape, Hackman created places for the eye to rest, such as the old spring house between the ponds. The Yoshino cherry trees, rimming the pond, were placed to highlight the view in springtime and, once planted, require little maintenance.

Close to the house, a sitting nook and a balcony were located in the kitchen garden. Here, Hackman built a wall to enclose the space and put in an antique wrought iron gate. Below an existing walled arch, an Italian stone lion head spills water into the wishing well below. Walls are colored with climbing roses and honeysuckle. Because all the major rooms in the house overlook this intimate courtyard, she designed it as a formal parterre garden with pea-gravel paths outlining the four stone-edged planting beds. To have four-season interest, she used dwarf boxwood hedges and placed topiary in the middle of each quadrant. In summer, herbs including chive, rosemary, and sage fill out the beds.

What made this project particularly satisfying for Hackman was her relationship with her client, who understood the value of this historic landscape and trusted Hackman to make the right decisions to preserve its natural beauty.

STONELEIGH FARM

129

STONELEIGH FARM

WALSH-SHERIDAN GARDEN

Lewes, Delaware   Scott Brinitzer, Scott Brinitzer Design Associates

"It was a puzzle," says Scott Brinitzer, describing the layout of this garden that angles back at 45-degrees from an old ship pilot's house through a series of outdoor living spaces to a contemplative garden at the rear. "The site plan is based on the original alignment of an old railroad track and nothing lines up with the house." Since the sight line from the back of the house is of the neighbor's yard to the left, Brinitzer borrowed a view of their park-like garden that included 150-year-old boxwood and he opened up the property so a serene shady back garden could be shared.

Behind the house and along a new addition, Brinitzer designed a series of diagonal garden rooms that keep adjusting to the right. From the dining terrace, the garden swings into a cozy living room with fireplace before it ducks under a breezeway with a fountain surrounded by an herb garden. Beyond a gated arbor lies the spa and then the pool with a backdrop of a sandstone water-trough fountain. A spring house beside the fountain serves as a folly with a gate that opens into the shared garden. Another variable: all these built garden features had to be setback at least ten feet from property lines.

To blend the 1836 house with the new elements, Brinitzer followed the simple lines of house, reproducing the classic square columns from the front porch in the construction of the rose-covered pergola breezeway and added a copper roof to the Spring House. To link the various garden rooms together visually, hydrangeas were a common thread, starting with the row of 'Nikko Blue' hydrangeas that span the front of the house to a bank of oakleaf hydrangeas in the back. As for the details, Italy was the inspiration. The house, originally lime green, was painted a Tuscan gold as were the fireplace, spring house, and seat walls. Two sets of three Italian cypress punctuate the back landscape, and smaller Italian touches include terra cotta pots, tabletops and lots of lavender.

131

"In the summer months no one is ever inside," Brinitzer says. "Breakfast is taken by the fireplace and later everyone is in the pool, even the dogs." At the end of the day, the owners can sit on the front porch to watch the sunset or cross a road that bisects the property and head for the wilder, waterside garden and dock on the Rehoboth-Lewes Canal. Near the Delaware Bay, this perennial garden uses wind and salt tolerant plants, such as rosa rugosa, bee balm, and purple coneflower, and especially native grasses "to connect it to the greater landscape of the marshes." The liberal use of calamagrostis, pennisetum, and miscanthus in this garden bring added volume to the long flower borders and are tall enough to provide some privacy in this open setting by the water's edge.

SHERIDAN-WALSH GARDEN

134

SHERIDAN-WALSH GARDEN

WATER STREET ROOFTOP

Washington, D.C.   Lisa E. Delplace, Oehme, van Sweden & Associates, Inc.

Built on top of an electric power substation overlooking the Potomac, this rooftop meadow enhances views from the condominium building behind. Because most of the tenants experience the garden by looking down on it from above, the meadow was designed with abstract blocks of color that would play off each other and be a movable feast with four-season interest. In spring, the garden is a blush of yellow, followed by a series of different shades of greens until midsummer, when it vibrates from the brilliant blue of the Russian sage and the joyous yellow of the 'Goldstrum' rudbeckia. In the fall, the panicum with its tawny seed heads puts on a dance, and in winter the landscape becomes monochromatic.

To support such abundance, a sandwich of five materials was placed to protect the roof and promote plant growth, starting with a seamless waterproofing membrane to the top layer of an engineered lightweight soil that resembles volcanic rock. Since the original building structure had been designed to support additional stories, this green roof could accommodate a deeper planting medium—eight inches instead of the standard four—for bulbs and a wider selection of drought-tolerant perennials. Two shrubs, pink flowering carpet roses and chaste trees, were planted on top of the building's interior support columns where the soil could be mounded. Trellises attached to two sides of the building collect excess water into downspouts and support vines covering the brick walls.

Like all green roofs, this one reduces the amount of heat, increases moisture and oxygen in the air, and helps reduce storm runoff. Since there is no access to this roof, birds that don't nest in trees are protected here, like a pair of duck that moved in last year. Tenants have also seen goldfinches, Eastern meadowlarks, and indigo bunting, and during summer the population of butterflies explodes.

"We are recapturing an abandoned part of our urban centers, roofs that we have relegated to be utilitarian, forgetting how beautiful they can be," says Lisa Delplace. Sustainability and aesthetics play crucial roles, and she can see how the residents have taken advantage of the views and brought colors from the garden into their living spaces. "Even though they can't open their doors and walk into it, the garden is a part of their experience," says she. "They have adopted it as their own."

137

WATER STREET ROOFTOP

141

ROXANA AND ROBERT LORTON GARDEN

Tulsa, Oklahoma   Peter Cummin, Cummin Associates

"There are practically no great gardens in the world without walls," says British-born landscape architect and horticulturist Peter Cummin. At this site, which incorporated a twenty-one-foot drop in grade, he enclosed the property with stone walls and built an underlying skeleton of stone that connects a series of multileveled terraces and staircases with more walls. "In the end it all fit together like a jigsaw puzzle," he says.

To soften the weight of the walls, he broke up the face of the limestone with terra cotta tiles, attached pergolas and added lush plantings, in particular vigorous vines, such as wisteria, Boston ivy, and fleece vine. Cummin also always followed Russell Page's advice to over-plant and then edit later. Borrowing views of neighboring trees made the property appear much larger and interrupted the line along boundary walls.

The French-style manor house and the garden are linked by the palette of materials. Kansas limestone is used on the facade of the house and in the garden walls; terra cotta tiles, oak wood beams, and water features are recurring elements. Cummin chose a mortar with a course grain of sand to replicate the texture of the stone and as it set, it was brushed to help age the walls.

143

If Cummin has a guiding principle, it is that "things should look like they have always been there." Here, antique cobblestones recycled from beneath Chicago streets create a warm, wheel-weathered patina in the entrance courtyard. Smooth bluestone surrounding the stone fountain adds coolness and a contrasting texture against the cobblestones. Small patches of dwarf mondo grass soften the hardscaping as well. A triple-deep formation of cloud-shaped boxwood sweeps along the front of the house, providing yearlong interest, as do the 'Halka' zelkova trees, planted on either side of the front door to echo the triangular shape of the window peaks.

Behind the house, the terraces unfold all the way across the back to Pistachio trees. Three staircases lead down to a great lawn, a pool, and a guesthouse. In one terraced room an iron Victorian fountain, chosen for its dark color and delicacy of size, runs from an octagonal bluestone pool along a rill that drops over a ledge into a grotto swimming pool below. Finding the right fountain took time, because "scale always needs to be right," adds Cummin. This garden has an English feel with an Oklahoma slant, which means that more drought tolerant plants, shrubs, and trees like lantana, butterfly bush, and crepe myrtles are used in place of traditional English plants.

LORTON CUMMIN

146

HAYS COUNTY GARDEN

Texas   Bill Bauer, Gardens

Bring water into an arid Texas environment and wildlife will follow. After Bill Bauer poured concrete for a pair of ponds and filled the basins, literally hundreds of frogs moved in. Birds came later, to bathe and drink, but when fish were added to the ponds, no one had imagined the next sighting: a Great Blue Heron dunking its head into the water and flying off with a blue-spotted goldfish in its beak.

All this activity is part of the design intent: to create a formal terrace set up with fountain ponds running parallel to the ranch house that would reflect the sky and become an active part of the two-and-a-half acre garden. Since the site was long and narrow, for Bauer, "It was all about setting up an entry sequence where the geometry made sense in front of the house." He accomplished that by layering the design into a maze of repeated forms and patterns between the clipped English boxwood, pea-gravel paths, and limestone-capped pond walls. The flat-topped boxwood hedges abut the ponds, which mirror their volume and height.

Other linear elements include the vertical lines of four Italian cypress set on either side of the wide staircase and the long line of white-flowering 'Natchez' crepe myrtles that leads into a circle paved in a basket-weave pattern of brick with lines of limestone radiating out from the center. Grayish-white block limestone walls and huge arborvitae define the terrace, which has endless views of the scrubby grasslands of Texas cattle country.

149

Behind the house, a folly by the pool is a gateway to a natural garden full of native plants, including Mexican feather grass, and architectural plants such as the spiky blue-tinged desert spoon. Outside the fenced areas and in the front terrace, it was important to choose deer-resistant plants. Inside the fenced back garden, a generous staircase leads down to a pea-gravel patio shaded by a canopy of live oak. From there, a circular path follows a sweep of cottage-style perennials bordering the yard.

Tuscany, with its similar soil type, geology, and weather patterns, served as a guide for translating this garden's classical framework into the vernacular of Texas. Handmade terra cotta pots from Florence and a huge antique copper urn serve as focal points, but the materials are mostly local, like the Texas chopped limestone used in the retaining walls and for the steps in the rear garden. Describing the balance between formality and the harsh landscape, Bauer says, "There was a crudeness with some of the stones we used. There was always this rustic part playing off the refined."

150

HAYS COUNTY GARDEN

153

HAYS COUNTY GARDEN

154

HAYS COUNTY GARDEN

A SCULPTURE GARDEN

Oklahoma   Bruce Berger, Armstrong/Berger Inc.

Bold gestures against a plain background, large blocks of color used to create a sense of space, and a minimal color palette—these elements could be used to describe modern art, but they also apply to this Oklahoma garden, made for a couple who collects contemporary sculpture. Besides the traditional functions of a garden as a place to connect to nature and to provide outdoor living space, this garden also serves as an art gallery, a park-like setting to display the collection, which includes work by Alexander Calder, Ellsworth Kelly, and Frank Stella.

This five-acre property, bordered by a green wall of towering hollies, needed to accommodate a range of events. "The goal was a garden that felt intimate for the owners and their family, but one where they could also entertain large groups," says Bruce Berger. Using subtle grade changes, Berger was able to visually divide the large terrace space in the back of the house into smaller, more personal spaces near the house for the couple. Green panels of wisteria and silvery elaeagnus growing up the sides of the putty-colored brick give the space a cool, soft look, even on a hot summer day, and the standard crepe myrtles gently screen the rest of the backyard, while providing shade and adding sculptural interest of their own with their smooth, mottled trunks.

Color in this garden plays three major notes: the earthy ochre tones of the enormous slabs of Hackett fieldstone used for retaining walls; cool-colored Pennsylvania bluestone used for paving; and the greens of trees, shrubs, and lawns that hold everything together. This minimal palette, along with an uncluttered design and the architectural use of plant materials, gives the garden a very contemporary feel. Terrace furniture is painted to match the bluestone, and paving itself was built with very tight joints to avoid introducing another pattern. Long, horizontal blocks of Wintergreen boxwood delineate outdoor spaces in a grid of terrace and lawn panels.

At the front of the house, in the center of the motor court is a dramatic red sculpture by Joel Shapiro. To line the motor court, Berger and his clients debated between Claudia Wannamaker magnolias and some deciduous trees. Berger advised that the deciduous trees would be nice, but the magnolias would be a bold gesture. The clients did not hesitate: "Let's go with the bold."

157

A SCULPTURE GARDEN

161

A SCULPTURE GARDEN

A HILL COUNTRY GARDEN

Austin, Texas   James deGrey David, David/Peese Design

Like all things Texan, this garden in the hill country has to be tough to survive the harsh conditions of alkaline soil, arid climate, and precipitous terrain. The topography of the site on the slopes of a ravine creates dramatic views and dictates a design that includes paths, steppingstones, and stairs up and down the steep hillside.

The most dramatic is a sixteen-foot-wide limestone staircase bisected by a runnel that carries rainwater down to a koi pond. "I didn't want to be stingy," says James David of the generous proportions he assigns his garden architecture. He also did not want to give away the delight of discovery. "I really plan how one space leads to another and how to close spaces down so you don't see too much until you reach it," he adds. Along the stairway, he used high clipped 'Will Fleming' yaupon holly hedges to keep the focus straight ahead to the pond sited on a creek bed and planted with lilies and lotuses.

"I've tried to make a garden that is influenced by lots of places, but is not necessarily of any of those places," David says. This is a Texas garden, taking its cues from the climate, region, architecture and plant material. Still there are many cues from the Mediterranean (the Italian cypress great lawn), Spain (the grand staircase), and France (the boxwood parterre garden). Indonesian teak canoes may lead the eye toward the urn at the edge of the ravine or Florentine pots may hold prickly pear cacti, but all are placed within a native woodland habitat. It is the drought-hardy trees such as the sculptural live oaks, the Mexican buckeye, and the cedar elms throughout the garden that provide its shady canopy.

In a scorching climate with little rain, David added more native trees, such as madrone, lacey oaks, and spice bush (Lindera benzoin). Since he could not depend on flowers, he chose plants for the texture, shape and the color of their foliage, including cacti, yucca, echinopsis, succulents, and sedums.

And it wouldn't be a Texas garden without a great space to barbecue. David created an outdoor dining room with modern, reddish rubber chairs and a plank-board table and placed it on axis to a classical dovecote constructed using methods by Germans who settled the area in the early nineteenth century.

165

A HILL COUNTRY GARDEN

CHARLES GRAVES GARDEN

Charleston, South Carolina   Robert Chesnut, Robert Chesnut Landscape Architect

Robert Chesnut is a firm believer in integrating house and garden: "I convert windows to doors and I create openings into garden rooms because my philosophy is if it's too far away or too hard to reach people won't bother to go out." Here each of the five distinct and interlocking garden rooms have easy access from the house and from one to another. All are furnished with swings, benches, tables and chairs because, as Chestnut says, "If you don't have seating in every garden, people won't use it."

The design leads gracefully from a parterre entry court to an old brick terrace with a swimming pool to a kitchen garden full of herbs and flowers. Behind these gardens is a sunken parking court hidden from sight by one of the oldest crepe myrtles in Charleston. On a raised formal oval lawn a circular fountain shoots up a plume of spray in front of a petite pavilion. At night, the pavilion, on axis with the columns of the porch, becomes a focal point lit up against the night sky. Chestnut insists on night lighting in his gardens to create a different and lively effect—a crepe myrtle becomes a sinuous sculpture etched in light and water features sparkle, for example.

In this temperate climate the garden becomes an extension of the house. Surrounding the pool terrace are four separate seating areas. To the left of the porch is a single teak bench placed against the house with climbing 'New Dawn' roses stitched into the pink stucco wall. Against this wall there are also espaliered apple trees and one exuberantly planted, wide window box. At the far end of the pool is a round table with chairs, and to the right is a shallow pergola wrapped in Confederate jasmine and more roses to provide much needed shade. Back on the piazza, the long, narrow porch, there is one more seating area with a marble table and ornate wrought iron chairs. Chesnut painted the pool a dark charcoal gray so at night it becomes a reflecting pool mirroring the quartet of reproduction Frank Lloyd Wright limestone urns planted with boxwood. For larger parties, the parking court, essential in the historic district, functions as an intimate space for cocktails or dining.

"My gardens are very axial," Chesnut says of his strong architectural and well-proportioned designs, which feature straight paths, topiary, low clipped hedges, and parterres. "I like symmetry. I like balance."

173

CHARLES GRAVES GARDEN

177

KIAWAH ISLAND GARDEN

South Carolina   John Tarkany, DesignWorks

Working on a spit of unspoiled maritime forest on a barrier island surrounded by salt marshes, John Tarkany was charged with leaving as "light a footprint on the land" as possible. This meant no lawn, no increased runoff, a soft surface driveway, and embellishing what nature had already created in this unique ecological environment off the coast of South Carolina.

At the back of the property and along either side of the house, Tarkany integrated new natives back into existing patterns of indigenous plants that thrive in this hot and humid climate. He introduced more yaupon hollies into natural drifts and added clumps of palms where a grove had stood before Hurricane Hugo to ensure that this "native landscape looks like it was created by nature and not a landscape architect." Sticking to natives—live oaks, sweet grass and saw palmettos—meant being faithful to the true horticultural character of the place. The subtropical climate allowed Tarkany to use eight different kinds of palms from sabal palmettos to sago and needle palms.

Since the land mass was so narrow by the road in front of the house, Tarkany says, "We had to establish a sense of privacy and seclusion quickly." To design for instant maturity, he upsized shrubs, palms, and trees so that the landscape would become established in a three to five year time span. Using mature specimens—oaks and magnolias—would also make the house appear smaller surrounded by large trees that would soften the roofline. He chose the heavy-blooming 'Claudia Wannamaker' magnolia, known for its pyramidal shape and its glossy green and brown-backed leaves, to make a bold impact in the landscape. Live oaks were chosen for their sculptural aesthetic and for their strength during hurricanes. Two massive Pindo Palms on either side of the porte cochere frame the entrance with silver fronds.

179

That sense of a hidden sanctuary in front provides an interesting visual contrast with the rear, which has a panoramic view of the marsh. "Views are best when you are looking past something out to something else," Tarkany explains, describing how a glimpse across the vast marshes to the Kiawah River becomes livelier when framed between two palms or under the branches of a live oak. Similarly the windows of the house, the infinity pool, and the guardrails on the deck are all positioned so that no element will interfere with the 180-degree sweep over the landscape. Since it's pitch black at night on Kiawah, a low-voltage lighting system was installed for a soft, moonlight effect on the deck. But to have the house recede into the landscape, only trees on the property were lit up from below.

KIAWAH ISLAND GARDEN

ANNE AND JACKSON WARD GARDEN

Coral Gables, Florida   Raymond Jungles, Raymond Jungles Landscape Architecture

This striking landscape of man-made water features originated with a unique client request: accommodations for a five-hundred-pound pet hog named Virginia. "After we made her grotto, we realized we had really started something," says Jungles, who went on to excavate a lake, a stream, a pond basin, and a sinkhole from the Miami oolite bedrock beneath two acres of lawn. None of this would have been possible if the site had not been situated on the region's highest ridge. A twenty-foot drop in grade provided an unparalleled opportunity for drama and scale with bluffs dangling above grottos and waterfalls spilling in deep pools.

Much of the limestone was saved. Monolithic chunks of stone, removed block-by-block, were stacked in various places within the garden as organic sculptures and to screen views of eight adjacent properties. For Jungles the garden was a breakthrough project. "We developed a whole new language in the way we sculpted the stone and created land forms," he says. "The use of native Florida materials brought about a truly regional garden style." This wasn't accomplished by following a detailed set of plans, but by working daily with his clients, imagining what the space could become.

Around the bluffs, narrow paths wind through bamboo groves and underneath rustling palms. The floor of an old swimming pool became an intimate terrace, and steps carved from the rock lead to quiet seating areas with views of the lake where Jungles sculpted massive "floating islands" by cutting around the boulders and leaving these landforms in place. The ponds create large openings to the sky, which in turn become a part of the garden canvas as the sky is reflected in the various bodies of water. The draw of water brings more life into the garden from the migratory songbirds—warblers and flycatchers—to the Everglades birds—herons and egrets—that roost nearby.

What has evolved is a timeless landscape that is reminiscent of nearby Matheson Hammock Park, fulfilling the owner's original wish. The white limestone walls have faded into a soft green and everything is buried in vegetation. "Anytime you put oxygen and sunlight into a space, you start getting life," says Jungles. The spores of the maidenhair ferns planted on the moist rock face quickly caught hold and now cover twice the area, and around the lake, pond apple and red mangrove grow in the water table that rises and falls with the tide. Indigenous plants such as the silver saw palmetto provide a lush under story and exotic trees, including kapok and Talipot, Bailey and Oil palms, add to its primeval character.

"This was more of an art project than any kind of a reconstruction," says Jungles. "You can tell the hand of man, yet it feels very natural."

186

ANNE AND JACKSON WARD GARDEN

189

191

ANNE AND JACKSON WARD GARDEN

ANNE AND JACKSON WARD GARDEN

SIMMONS GARDEN

Charleston, South Carolina   Sheila Wertimer, Wertimer & Associates

Tucked behind wrought iron gates in the historic district are the secret gardens of Charleston, but not all are traditional designs. In this chic, modern Italian courtyard garden, Sheila Wertimer substituted creeping fig for climbing roses and stands of Japanese black bamboo for banks of blue mophead hydrangeas.

To create a welcoming entryway, she added a 60-foot-long French limestone walk, turning the narrow space, just twelve feet across, into an elegant allée, and lined it with pleached and pollarded sycamores and autumn ferns. "I wanted a very simple palette of plants that had real punch visually that brought you within the garden immediately," says Wertimer. By limiting the number of plants to two, the focus remains on the unembellished pleasures of the trees and their peeling bark with the feathery ferns at their feet. Both plants work year round, with the trees providing shade in the hot summer months; after the leaves drop in winter, a soft, dappled light fills the graceful space.

The walkway leads to a sunny, intimate outdoor living space between the main house and a guesthouse. There, Wertimer made the 40-by-40 foot courtyard appear larger by using paving materials to organize it into three spaces: a terra cotta tiled seating area, a continuation of the creamy limestone pathway, and a pool. She chose a French-gray color for the bottom to make it look more like a reflecting pool, and she designed a limestone rim, which is raised on one side for seating.

197

Perimeter plantings with texture and vertical lines add drama and scale. Japanese timber bamboo was selected for its strokes of muted color and its repetitive silhouette. The bamboo is limbed up to only leaf out above the brick wall to enhance privacy. To keep it from spreading, the bamboo is planted in two-and-a-half-feet deep steel-lined troughs. Bold, broad-leafed Chinese fan palm are used as accents in the beds, and creeping fig vine softens the nineteenth-century brick boundary walls.

Interlocking grillwork on the backdoor resembles fish, and all the 1950s vintage wrought iron furniture mimics the delicate metalwork on the balconies overlooking the courtyard. Pots become an important design element in this uncluttered garden. The overscaled pots beside the pool were planted with orange trees and rosemary, a reference to the Italian inspiration of this garden.

SIMMONS GARDEN

SIMMONS GARDEN

CAMINITO AL MAR

Golden Beach, Florida   Raymond Jungles, Raymond Jungles Landscape Architecture

When Raymond Jungles designs his vibrant tropical gardens, his goal is a sense of "a clearing in the woods, of secluded space tucked away in nature." In this garden on Golden Beach, Jungles wrapped a narrow lot in a cocoon of tropical plants to protect the site from a busy road and houses on each side. Layering contrasting plants of different size, shape, color and texture, he erased all thoughts of the external world and allowed nothing to be revealed outside its borders except the Atlantic Ocean.

A line of towering trees, pigeon plum, Bismarckia and sabal palms, shields the entrance, and a stand of "leaning palms" juts out into the motor court to minimize its mass and to soften its brick edges. Intricate stainless steel gates and an arbor over the garage façade, designed by Mauricio Del Valle, connect the front with the back and are a reminder of how the trade winds sway the grasses on this oceanfront property. Jungles popped up palms through the arbor to create bold interruptions between it and the garage.

In the entrance garden, a broad travertine walkway rises gently past the front door to the back gate where there is a spectacular view of the ocean framed through a bottle palm across an infinity-edged pool. Between the house and the property wall, there are five built elements: the walk, a ridged, black water rill that spills over two falls, and three narrow garden beds that create bands of solids and voids. Low plants, such as dwarf mondo grass and Paurotis palm, cover the bed in front of the rill and Jungles used Mexican breadfruit, Coconut and Florida silver palms to break up the white wall of the house. At night, fiber optic lights in the rill flicker like fireflies under the rippling water.

203

"I always think about how to make walls catch light to animate space," Jungles explains. The outdoor lighting creates shadow play against the walls both inside and out with plants caught in sea breezes or water moving across surfaces. Travertine paving from the pathway and terrace continues inside as the flooring of the house, blurring the distinction between inside and outside. Floor-to-ceiling windows add to a smooth transition. In a narrow side yard where the living room windows were only ten feet from a neighbor's wall, there is a viewing shelf for unique plant specimens and found objects, which adds an informal gallery space and screens the view of next door.

Jungles was delighted to find, when designing the pool, that tile his client had selected echoed the gradations of color, from turquoise to dark blue, in the ocean beyond. To keep the sand from blowing into the pool and to add more native habitat for birds, crabs, and sea turtles, Jungles covered the dunes with a beach meadow of agaves, yuccas, and beach sunflower.

CAMINITO AL MAR

207

CAMINITO AL MAR

First, I'd like to thank the garden owners who opened up their exquisite gardens to me and tolerated how early in the morning I arrived and how late in the evening I left. Their generosity allows garden lovers a glimpse into the private sanctuaries that are true collaborations between owner and designer. I hope they know how thankful I always was for the early morning cups of hot coffee and the late afternoon glasses of ice-cold drinks.

I am grateful to the landscape architects and gardens designers who regularly entrust me with their reputations when they commission me to photograph their creations. Their talent makes my work a delight. I appreciate the time they spent making preparations for the gardens to be photographed, moving furniture, turning off automatic watering systems or running out to a local nursery to buy a last-minute replacement for a struggling shrub. They would walk me through the spaces to help me understand what was accomplished there, sometimes weeding or pruning along the way, and they took the time to thoughtfully answer many questions about their creative process.

The idea for this book has been a subject of discussion between my wife, Darcy Trick, and me for a while, but it was during a conversation with Andrea Monfried, editorial director at the Monacelli Press, that she had the vision to see the possibility of creating this book. Thanks so much, Andrea. A big thanks to my editor, Elizabeth White, who patiently worked with me on the text, and the designer, Susan Evans, who, I could tell from the first sample layouts, spoke an exciting visual language that matched up beautifully with my photographs.

I am indebted to the magazines in which some of the gardens in this book first appeared, particularly *Southern Accents*, *Garden Design*, *Home and Design*, *American Style* and *Gardens Illustrated*, and their editors: Karen Carroll, Lindsay Bierman, Lydia Somerville, Nancy Staab, Frances MacDougall, Bill Marken, Joanna Fortnam, Sarah Kinbar, Donna Dorian, Sharon Dan, Hope Daniels, Juliet Roberts, and Dean Riddle.

Life as a freelancer can be a solitary business, but the ASMP and the Garden Writers' Association have given me communities of fellow professionals to discuss business issues, solve technical problems, or to share successes. Through the GWA I met garden photographers Alan and Linda Detrick. Alan and I have since become brothers in arms, sharing the many ups and downs of our chosen profession and teaching workshops together. In the days before digital, the photo lab was a meeting place for photographers; that place for me was Capital Color. The owner, Mike Langford, was perfectly obsessive about the quality of his film processing, but he still took time to be a friend. At Pro Photo, brothers Dick and Sebouh Baghdassarian have been taking expert care of my camera equipment for more than thirty years.

My mother, Charlotte, and my late father, Roger Sr., have always been supportive of my decision to become a photographer, even though I made up my mind while in architecture school. They have always been my most ardent fans, collecting copies of every photograph published. Their encouragement gave me the confidence to move forward. Today, my mother's love and support still helps to keep me going. When I did transfer from the architecture program to the art department at Notre Dame, I was lucky to have a wonderful and wise teacher, Richard Stevens, who encouraged me to follow my own path of self-expression through my photography.

Thanks, Kate, for all your work transcribing twenty-five hours of phone interviews with the designers, even though the language of horticulture and garden design are not yet part of your daily life. Darcy, my wife and partner for thirty-five years, has the ambiguous fortune to live with a freelance photographer. It's not all exotic locations and expense accounts. For this project, she was the engine pulling the train up the mountain—without her, this book would simply not have existed. Indeed, without her, my career as a garden photographer would not have been possible. She gave me the confidence to begin crafting texts for this book. With her background in newspaper reporting and an omnivorous appetite for fiction, Darcy taught me to think about the word, and therefore the world, more deeply than I ever would have on my own. Anything I may have learned about writing has come from her influence and her patience in working with me to revise anything I write again and again until it becomes clear. Not a word in these pages has escaped her scrutiny.